Idiot

SWEAR WORD

COLORING BOOK

for Parents

COLOR TEST PAGE

COLOR TEST PAGE

Bullshit

FUCK

Piss Off

Asshole

Bitch

SLUT

Whore

Bastard

Damn

Shitballs

Sugartits

Twat
Waffle

Be happy

Piss Flaps

Bollocks

CRAP

Fuckwit

www.ingramcontent.com/pod-product-compliance
Lightning Source LLC
Chambersburg PA
CBHW081127280526
45787CB00007B/3004
* 9 7 8 1 5 3 5 0 2 2 0 4 0 *